SIMPLE TI̶̶̶̶
THE KITCHEN

Member of the
Evangelical Christian
Publishers Association

Printed in the United States of America.

SIMPLE TIPS FOR
THE KITCHEN

BARBOUR
PUBLISHING

There is no doubt that it is around the family and the home that all the greatest virtues, the most dominating virtues of human society, are created, strengthened, and maintained.

WINSTON CHURCHILL

LOVELY MEMORIES

Kitchens aren't just for creating palate-pleasing meals. . . .
Maybe even more important are some of the
loveliest memories that are created there.

● ● ●

SALTY SOUP?

Salt is a wonderful flavor enhancer, but too much of it can spoil an entire recipe. If your soup ends up too salty, cut a raw potato or turnip into large chunks and drop the chunks into the soup to cook for several minutes. The chunks will naturally absorb the salt and can be removed before serving.

BACON IN A FLASH

Cook up a pound of bacon until done but not crisped.
When cooled and drained of fat, cut or crumble the
bacon and store it in a freezer container. It can then
be added quickly to a casserole or salad.

● ● ●

Part of the secret of success in life is to eat what you like and let the food fight it out inside.

MARK TWAIN

SAY GOOD-BYE TO
TOMATO STAINS

Protect your storage containers from unsightly tomato stains
by spraying them with cooking oil before filling them.

● ● ●

A BOILED-OVER MESS

It is said that a watched pot never boils—but an unattended pot can easily boil over and create a cleaning challenge. Try rubbing butter around the top few inches of your pot to prevent boiled-over mishaps.

DON'T CRY OVER ONIONS

Here are some great tear-free solutions for handling onions:

- Keep onions in the refrigerator. Warm onions easily release their fumes.
- Peel and cut onions under running water.
- Don't cut off the "bloom" end of the onion—where the fumes are stored.

NO-MESS DEVILED EGGS

One no-mess method for deviling your eggs is to place
your filling ingredients into a plastic bag.
Massage the bag to mix; then cut a small hole
in one corner of the bag. Squeeze the filling
out of the bag and directly into the hollows of
the egg whites.

DO MORE WITH YOUR EGG SLICER

An egg slicer works great for slicing strawberries, mushrooms, boiled potatoes, cooked and peeled beets, and much more.

● ● ●

ICE CUBE CREATIVITY

Fill ice cube trays with punch (or iced tea, iced coffee, juice, etc.) and then freeze. These ice cubes won't water down your beverages.

KITCHEN TIME—GOD TIME!

Make your kitchen time your "God time." Who says
you can't talk with God while you're cooking at the
stove or standing at the sink rinsing dishes?

● ● ●

STICKY MESS CLEANUP

When measuring corn syrup, first spray your measuring cup with cooking oil. The syrup will come out easily and cleanup will be fast. This also works well for peanut butter, marshmallow cream, honey, and molasses.

I'M BLESSED!

Lord, thank You for my home—and for my kitchen,
where I am able to create tasty meals for my family.
You have provided me with so much, and I often forget
how blessed I am. I praise You, Lord. Amen.

Be content with what you have.
HEBREWS 13:5

● ● ●

EASY EGG SEPARATION

A good trick for separating egg white from the yolk is to break the egg into a funnel held over a small bowl. The white will pass through the funnel while the yolk remains suspended at the top.

QUICK-RISE TRICK
FOR BREAD DOUGH

The dishwasher is a great place for letting bread dough rise.
Place the dough in a bowl and cover with a towel.
Set the bowl on the bottom rack of the dishwasher
and then turn on the dishwasher's dry heat cycle.
The warm, moist air is perfect for a quick rise.

● ● ●

FUDGE FIX

Fudge doesn't come out of the pan well, so line your pan either with aluminum foil or waxed paper first. Form the foil to your pan and then pour in the fudge. When the fudge has cooled, you can easily lift it from the pan and place it on a cutting board before slicing it into squares.

GOOD MESSES

Find you're often distressed over a messy kitchen? Instead of
focusing on the yucky part of cleanup, remember that the dirty
pots and pans, the sticky table, and the crumbs on the floor
all mean that you have a family who needs your love and care.
Now doesn't that make it all worthwhile?

● ● ●

NEW DISHES

Tired of preparing the same dishes all the time? Make it a priority to try a new recipe each week. Not only will you expand your culinary skills, but chances are there's a new family favorite waiting to make an appearance on your table.

INSTANT GIFT!

Attach brewing instructions to a jarful of
cappuccino mix and give as a gift to a friend.

● ● ●

TASTIER BREAD AND ROLLS

Enhance a plain roll or slice of bread with extra flavor.
Soften a stick of butter then whip in your
choice of garlic, rosemary, lemon juice, or
honey.

KIDS IN THE KITCHEN

Allow your kids to get involved in the kitchen.
Invite them to help you measure and add in the ingredients
while you manage the hot oven. It's a win-win situation.
They'll be proud of their creation. . .and you'll enjoy
the quality time spent with your kids!

● ● ●

The kitchen is the great laboratory
of the household.

FROM *THE BOOK OF HOUSEHOLD MANAGEMENT*
BY ISABELLA BEETON

BETTER-TASTING CHEESE BALLS

A cheese ball seasons better if made a day in advance.

● ● ●

● ● ●

SPIRIT LIFTER

Invite a friend over for coffee or tea. You'll find that the
conversation and company will lift your spirit
and rejuvenate your soul.

REAL SMOOTH!

Experiment with different flavors of juice concentrate to create your own original smoothies. Get really creative and mix two unique juice concentrates with ice cream and milk. You might just discover a hidden talent while experimenting with these drink concoctions!

● ● ●

UNEXPECTED COMPANY?
NO PROBLEM!

Don't have time to bake for unexpected
company? Sweet breads freeze well. When the
bread is cool, wrap it tightly in aluminum foil
and place the loaf in a resealable freezer bag.
Frozen sweet breads will keep for several months.

EASY PREP FOR BISCUITS

Premeasure all dry ingredients and place the amount for one recipe into individual bags for easy preparation later.

● ● ●

BAKING PRODUCTS THAT LAST

Baking products can be expensive, and you don't want anything to go to waste. If you don't bake very often or like to buy your baking ingredients in bulk, you can keep many products like baking chocolate, baking chips, flour, nuts, dried fruits, butter, marshmallows, and cream cheese in the freezer until you are ready to use them.

DUST YOUR PANS WITH COCOA

If you prepare your pan with flour, you could end up with an unsightly white residue on your cake. Try dusting pans with cocoa instead of flour when you're baking a chocolate dessert.

● ● ●

FOR SOMEONE SPECIAL

A simple gift idea for someone special: Insert a coupon for one of your signature desserts inside a card.

CREAMIER PUDDING

For a richer, creamier pudding, use canned
evaporated milk instead of regular whole milk.

● ● ●

PAPER TOWEL MAGIC

Have you ever created a mess when you've tried to put a cover over a frosted cake? When you don't have a raised lid for your cake pan, lay a paper towel over the top instead. The frosting will stick at first, but soon the oils in the frosting will soak into the towel, and when you are ready to remove the paper towel, your frosting won't be pulled from the cake.

KITCHEN KINDNESS

A simple kindness, like baking an extra cake and giving it
away to a neighbor, has the potential to make a big impact.
Reaching out to others with your culinary creations
leaves lasting imprints on their hearts.

● ● ●

COOKIE PAINT

For lots of fun and great results, let your kids "paint"
their own cookies. Make paint by mixing
food coloring with egg yolks. Use brand-new
paintbrushes and let the kids paint pictures on
the cookies before baking. After baking, the
colors will come out bright and glossy.

DROP COOKIES IN A FLASH

When making drop cookies, make a double batch.
Form the extra dough into cookie-sized balls and freeze them
on a cookie sheet. Once frozen, place the dough balls into
labeled resealable bags and store in the freezer. Later, you can
remove only the number of cookies you need to bake. No need
for thawing. Now you can have a variety of cookies ready to
bake for unexpected guests or for quick, tasty gifts.

FRESH EGGS?

Are your eggs fresh? To determine freshness, immerse each egg in a pan of cool, salted water. If it sinks, it is fresh; if it floats on the surface, throw it out.

COOKIE MAILING

Soft cookies are better for mailing than crisp ones.

● ● ●

FRESH LEMON JUICE

When juicing a lemon, bring it to room temperature and roll it under your palm along the counter before cutting and squeezing. This action will release the most juice.

NO-STICK DOUGH

To keep dough from sticking to your rolling pin, try using
nylon. Take a clean, never-worn knee-high stocking and
cut off the toe. Slide the nylon over your rolling pin.
The nylon helps hold an even layer of flour on the
pin so you can easily flatten moist dough.

● ● ●

DIP CHILLERS

To keep your dips chilled at a party, choose two
complementary glass bowls—one larger than
the other. Fill the larger bowl with ice chips.
Fill the smaller bowl with your dip and set the
bowl down into the ice.

FRUIT BOWL CREATIVITY

A "real" fruit bowl makes a fanciful serving dish for your fruit dip. Cut a whole fresh pineapple lengthwise—leaving the green top on. Hollow out the fruit, leaving a thick wall. Fill the bowl with dip. Other rind fruits, such as oranges, lemons, and cantaloupe, also make good serving bowls.

● ● ●

PUNCH BOWL ISLAND

When you want ice in your punch bowl without a lot of
extra water, try freezing all or part of your punch
ingredients into ice cubes or one large chunk.
The ice floats in the center of the punch bowl
like an island, and it melts slowly. No worry
about this ice cube getting into individual glasses.

*I will tell of the kindnesses of the LORD,
the deeds for which he is to be praised,
according to all the LORD has done for us —
yes, the many good things he has done.*

ISAIAH 63:7

● ● ●

GIVE THANKS

Make a habit of thanking the Lord before each meal. After all, He's the one who's given us such abundance; because of His goodness, we can eat our fill and not go hungry each night. Take turns giving thanks around the dinner table. Have each family member participate. Prepare to be amazed at how the Lord has blessed each one of you.

FRESH PUMPKIN

Wash a pumpkin thoroughly, then cut it in half.
Don't remove the seeds and pulp; place the meat side
down in a large cake pan. Bake in a 300-degree oven
until you can easily pierce the skin with a fork. The time
will vary with the size of your pumpkin. When cooled,
drain the juices and remove the skin and seeds.
Mash the pumpkin and use as you would canned pumpkin.

● ● ●

LOVE FROM YOUR KITCHEN

Share some love from your kitchen. Surprise your coworkers
with a breakfast snack. Bake up a coffee cake
and place it near the coffeepot at work.

QUICK AND EASY FLOUR CLEANUP

Before washing a bowl that had flour in it,
first rinse in cold water. Hot water causes
flour to gel and become harder to wash away.

● ● ●

GO BANANAS!

Bananas won't ripen in the refrigerator. They keep best in a paper bag at room temperature. If you don't get ripe bananas used up, divide them into one-cup portions and freeze them for later use.

FROSTED COOKIE FREEZE

When you want to freeze cookies that are frosted, place the cookies uncovered on a baking sheet in the freezer for a few hours. Then when you individually wrap the cookies in plastic wrap or stack the cookies in a container, you won't have to worry about the frosting sticking. When ready to use, simply remove the cookies from their container before they thaw.

● ● ●

ACTS OF LOVE

Lord, thank You for my children. May I be reminded that each
meal prepared, every kitchen cleanup, and each
trip to the grocery store are acts of love I may
pass along to my family. Amen.

MESSY BEATER CLEANUP

Messy beaters can easily be rinsed clean if you
leave them on the mixer and run them in a bowl
of hot water for approximately one minute.

● ● ●

NEED A GRAHAM CRACKER CRUST?

When you need a graham cracker crust,
put whole graham crackers in a large resealable
bag and use a rolling pin to crush the crackers
to fine crumbs.

DON'T WANT BROWN BANANAS?

To keep bananas from turning brown, dip them in lemon juice.

● ● ●

MESSY OVEN CLEANUP

If you forget to place a piece of foil under your fruit pie and the juice bubbles out of the pan while baking, sprinkle some baking soda on the spill and let it bake to a crispy crust that can be easily brushed away when cooled.

MIXING MEATLOAF

When mixing meatloaf, place all ingredients in a large resealable
bag. Close the bag and mash the ingredients together. Push the
meat into a log shape and roll it out of the bag into your baking
dish. Be sure to throw away the bag when you're finished.

● ● ●

FAMILY TIME

Before mealtime, spend a few moments with your family
while committing a scripture verse to heart.
First one to learn the verse doesn't have to help
with cleanup!

MESSY EGG CLEANUP

Egg-based foods can be hard to clean off plates and utensils.
Sprinkle the dishes with some salt right after the meal.
The salt reacts with the egg and makes for easier cleanup.

● ● ●

BAKING SODA PASTE

Cleaning up a greasy mess doesn't have to be a chore if you use this little trick: Sprinkle a generous amount of baking soda into your pan when you are done cooking; add a bit of water and blend to form a paste. Let your pan stand while you and your family enjoy a meal together. When you are ready to wash your pan, it will clean up fast. You won't believe the shine! (This little cleaning tip also works wonders on the stove top.)

BEING TOGETHER

If your family is prone to distraction during dinnertime,
turn off the TV, leave the radio off, don't answer the telephone...
Make a "no interruptions" rule at the dinner table
so you can focus on just being together.

● ● ●

HAMBURGERS IN NO TIME FLAT!

Hamburgers cook up faster when they're shaped a bit like a doughnut. After you form the meat into a patty, make a ¼-inch hole in the center. By the time the hamburger is cooked, the hole will have disappeared.

SPIRIT REFRESHERS

Let's face it. These days, it's difficult to find time for yourself. After you slide a dish into the oven, make the next half-hour "me" time. Read your Bible. . .pick up that new book you've been meaning to read. . .play a game with your kids. . .make a phone call to a friend you've been wanting to catch up with. . . talk to your husband about his day. . .take a catnap. However you choose to spend this time, you'll be refreshed— and looking forward to cooking your next meal!

● ● ●

SUGARCOAT IT

Try dusting your cake pans with regular sugar instead of flour. The mild, sweet coating on a cake is more appealing than lumpy flour.

QUICK RICE POT CLEANUP

After adding rice to the water, turn the burner to low,
cover the pot with a folded dish towel, and then
hold it in place with the pot's lid. As the rice cooks,
the towel absorbs the water and cleanup is a snap.

● ● ●

LETTUCE CORE

When cutting up a whole head of lettuce, always use this
nifty tip: To get the core out, just give the head's
core a whack down on the countertop. Then
give the core a twist, and it comes right out.

CRYSTALLIZED HONEY

Crystallization is a natural process for honey, but it doesn't mean you have to throw it out. Place the jar of honey in a pan of warm water and stir the honey until the crystals dissolve. You can also microwave the honey for thirty seconds, stir, and repeat for another thirty seconds until the crystals have dissolved.

● ● ●

WHAT'S FOR DINNER?

Make meal planning a family event. One day, you choose
what goes on the menu; then the rest of the
week, your family members can take turns
choosing the main course. Post the weekly
menu on a chalkboard or Dry-Erase board
in the kitchen. You'll find that everyone looks
forward to suppertime. . .and you'll rarely hear,
"What's for dinner?"

THIN SOUP?

Instant mashed potatoes can be added to soup to thicken it.
(To thin, add additional chicken broth.)

● ● ●

HOMEGROWN GIFTS

Give a living gift of a homegrown houseplant or herbs you've cultivated from seeds.

Take clippings from a hearty plant such as an ivy, philodendron, or spider plant. Start them in a tin, a clay pot, a coffee mug, an old boot, a lined basket, or any unique pot. Keep soil moist until rooted. Attach plant care instructions with a ribbon.

CHOCOLATE, CHOCOLATE, CHOCOLATE!

A good chocolate drink could always use...more chocolate! Custom-make your own stirring spoons. Dip a plastic spoon into melted chocolate. Allow it to set slightly, resting on waxed paper, and then fill the spoon with more melted chocolate. When the chocolate is cooled and completely set, you can wrap and give them to other chocolate lovers on your gift list.

● ● ●

EMPTY COFFEE CANS

Old coffee cans make great gift containers. Paint the outside of the can. Add a design with paint or permanent markers. You can also use stickers or glue on foam shapes, sequins, and ribbons. Decorate the lid with a piece of fabric.

NIFTY SUBSTITUTIONS

ALLSPICE—1 teaspoon allspice = ½ teaspoon cinnamon plus
½ teaspoon ground cloves

BAKING POWDER—1 teaspoon baking powder = ½ teaspoon
baking soda plus ⅝ teaspoon cream of tartar

BUTTERMILK—1 cup buttermilk = 1 cup milk plus 1 tablespoon
lemon juice or white vinegar (let stand 5 minutes
before using)

● ● ●

PERFECTLY ROUND COOKIES

When slicing logs of refrigerated cookie dough, roll the dough every other cut so the bottom of the log doesn't flatten. Each cookie will be perfectly round.

NIFTY SUBSTITUTIONS

BROWN SUGAR—½ cup brown sugar (firmly packed) = 1 cup white sugar or ½ cup white sugar plus 2 tablespoons molasses

CORNSTARCH— (for thickening) 1 tablespoon cornstarch = 2 tablespoons all-purpose flour or 2 tablespoons granular tapioca

CORN SYRUP—1 cup corn syrup = 1 cup sugar plus ¼ cup liquid or 1 cup honey (use whatever liquid is called for in recipe)

NIFTY NAPKIN RINGS

To make nifty napkin rings for your family dinner, start with a hodgepodge of old spoons and forks from family collections or flea markets. Use your hands to bend the pliable ones around a paper towel tube. Let the ends meet side by side, and you have a delightful napkin ring. Make an extra set for a gift.

NIFTY SUBSTITUTIONS

GARLIC—1 small clove fresh garlic = ⅛ teaspoon garlic powder

HERBS—1 tablespoon fresh-cut herbs = 1 teaspoon dried herbs

HONEY—1 cup honey = 1¼ cups sugar and ¼ cup liquid
(use whatever liquid is called for in recipe)

● ● ●

WARM HEARTS

A great way to warm hearts on cold winter days is to tell your loved ones how much they mean to you. That, along with a steaming mug of hot chocolate, can't be beat!

Above all, love each other deeply.
1 PETER 4:8

NIFTY SUBSTITUTIONS

LEMON JUICE—1 teaspoon lemon juice = ½ teaspoon vinegar

MUSTARD—1 teaspoon dry mustard = 1 tablespoon prepared mustard

ONION—1 medium onion = 1 tablespoon onion powder
       1 small onion = 1 tablespoon dried minced onion

● ● ●

DRESSING RECIPE IDEA

Bake dressing recipes in muffin tins. A pan of dressing muffins will bake at 350 degrees for 15 to 20 minutes and make perfectly-portioned servings for your feast.

NIFTY SUBSTITUTIONS

Self-rising flour—1 cup sifted self-rising flour = 1 cup sifted all-purpose flour plus, 1½ teaspoons baking powder and ½ teaspoon salt

Sour cream—1 cup sour cream = 1 cup plain yogurt or 1 cup cottage cheese pureed in blender with 1 tablespoon lemon juice and ⅓ cup butter

Unsweetened baking chocolate— 1 ounce unsweetened baking chocolate = 3 tablespoons unsweetened cocoa plus 1 tablespoon butter or shortening

CHERISHED RECIPE BOOKS

Use three-ring binders to create family cookbooks. Include recipes for all the family favorites with a brief bio and photo of the creator of each dish. These gifts will be cherished for years to come.

NIFTY SUBSTITUTIONS

VANILLA BEAN—½ bean = 1 tablespoon vanilla extract

WHIPPING CREAM—1 cup whipping cream, unwhipped =
2 cups whipped topping

WINE—1 cup wine = 1 cup grape, cranberry, apple juice, or
chicken broth

QUICK COOKIE COOL-DOWN

In the winter, use a table on your porch as a place to quickly cool down cookies and candies.

APRON FOR LITTLE HELPERS

An old shirt makes a quick apron for your little helper.
Use the arms to tie the shirt around the child's waist.

● ● ●

STICK SPAGHETTI IN IT!

When you need to test the "doneness" of a cake or bread and you don't have a cake-testing tool, use an uncooked piece of spaghetti. It is long enough to test your deepest baked goods.

PUT MARSHMALLOWS IN IT!

Keep brown sugar soft by placing two to three large marshmallows in the canister with the brown sugar.

● ● ●

SHINY PASTRY

For a professional brown and shiny finish on your pastry,
brush egg white onto the inside of your
piecrust before filling it and again on the top
before baking.

PIECRUST SAVER

To protect the edges of your piecrust from over-browning, grab a disposable aluminum pie pan. Cut out the bottom of the pan. The ring is perfect for setting over your baking pie during the last fourth of baking time.

● ● ●

COOLING RACKS FOR COOKIES

Old metal racks from worn-out refrigerators and ovens
make good cooling racks for cookies and
other baked goods. Their large size is great for
holiday baking sprees.

PINECONE CHEESE BALL

For a fun twist, create a pinecone out of your cheese ball.
Shape your cheese mixture into a cone. Use whole or sliced
almonds to cover the cheese ball in overlapping rows
like the rows on a pinecone.

● ● ●

JUST FOR TEA LOVERS

For the tea lover on your gift list, collect a variety of tea bags or loose tea, a tea ball strainer, a teacup, shortbread cookies, butter crackers, honey, and jam to fill a large teapot. Or place teapot and all in a basket lined with a tea towel.

EXTRA COUNTER SPACE

Counter space is often a precious commodity in a busy kitchen.
For a quick and handy extra countertop, set up your ironing
board and cover it with a plastic tablecloth.

● ● ●

FLAVOR ENHANCER

Create a wonderful enhancement for your meals. Soften a stick of real butter to room temperature. Mince ¼ cup of a fresh herb of your choice (basil, chive, oregano, rosemary, thyme). Blend the butter and herb, and store in an airtight container. Enjoy with breads and vegetables for up to three weeks.

FOR THE BIRDS

Don't forget the wild birds on those snowy days. Spread peanut
butter on a pinecone, then roll it in birdseed. Use a wire to hang
it on a tree. You can also cut an orange in half, scoop out the
fruit, and fill the rind with birdseed. It can be fashioned
into a basket that will hang from a tree limb.

● ● ●

DESIGNER COOKIES

Use a stencil or a lacy paper doily to easily decorate cakes, bars, and cookies. Place the stencil on the top of a warm cake, and sift powdered sugar or cocoa over all. Carefully remove the stencil, and you'll be left with a fantastic design.

PERFECT PEANUT
BUTTER COOKIES

For perfect crisscross patterns on top of your peanut butter
cookies, first wet the prongs of a table fork with milk.
Then dip the fork in white sugar and press into the
dough twice, forming a cross design.

● ● ●

CANNING JAR GIFTS

Fill a canning jar with colorful candies. Tie a ribbon and tag around the neck of the jar, and you have an instant gift. Add a note tag that says, "You are a real sweetie" or "I appreciate your sweet friendship." You could also fill a jar with small cookie cutters and attach your favorite sugar cookie recipe.

CANDY COOKING TERMINOLOGY

THREAD (230 degrees)—Candy will create a thin thread or ribbon when
dropped from a spoon. (Syrup)

SOFT BALL (234 degrees)—When dropped into water, candy will form into
a ball that is moldable when handled. (Fudge)

FIRM BALL (244 degrees)—This ball will hold a good shape but flatten
when pressed. (Caramel)

QUICK SPILL PICKUP!

When measuring dry ingredients, especially if children are
helping, chances are you'll wind up with a mess
on your countertop. Do your measuring over a
paper plate or a sheet of waxed paper. Spills can
then be picked up easily and returned to the
canister.

CANDY COOKING TERMINOLOGY

HARD BALL (250 degrees)—At this point, the ball is very firm and sticky. (Rock candy)

SOFT CRACK (270 degrees)—The ball will stretch into hard but not brittle threads. (Taffy)

HARD CRACK (300 degrees)—If you tap this ball against something, it will break into brittle pieces. (Peanut brittle)

● ● ●

TIME-OUT!

If you're overworked and overstressed, take a time-out and do absolutely nothing all by yourself. Savor this time and let the Lord speak to your heart.

EQUIVALENT PAN SIZES

- Use two 8-inch layer pans or 1½ to 2 dozen cupcakes in muffin tins.
- Use three 8-inch layer pans or two 9-inch square pans.
- Use one 9-inch layer pan or one 8-inch square pan.
- Use two 9-inch layer pans or one 9 x 13-inch pan or one 9-inch tube pan or two 8-inch square pans.
- Use one 5 x 9-inch loaf pan or two dozen cupcakes in muffin tins.

BLENDER CLEANUP

For a quick blender cleanup, fill ⅓ of the blender with hot water. Add a drop of dish detergent. Cover and turn on for a few seconds. Rinse and dry.

FRESH LEMON AND LIME
JUICE ALL YEAR

Did you know that lemons and limes can be frozen whole?
Then when you're in need of fruit juice, you can simply thaw
the lemon or lime in the microwave and squeeze out
fresh-tasting juice any time of the year.

● ● ●

HARD-BOILED EGG HELP

When boiling eggs, add a tablespoon of vinegar to the water to keep the eggs from cooking out if they crack. Also, remove from heat immediately and add cold water to the pan to cool them quickly. They will peel more easily.

PIZZA IDEA!

Make your kids mini "message" pizzas. Use toppings to create
words. For example, take chopped green pepper and place it so
it spells "Love you." Or create a personalized pizza by making
an initial with mushrooms. Your children will look forward to
the next special pizza you create just for them!

● ● ●

THAWING MEAT

To thaw meat at room temperature, place it on a metal pan. Metal conducts heat.

STALE BREAD TO THE RESCUE!

It is hard to drain off all the fat from ground beef without getting the meat mixed in. To soak up any remaining grease, dab cooked beef with a stale piece of bread or a bread heel.

● ● ●

ENJOY LIFE—OUTSIDE OF THE KITCHEN

Make cleanup a snap by washing pots and pans as soon as you're finished with them. The longer you let them sit, the harder it will be to get them clean and the more time you'll have to spend in the kitchen (when you could be out there enjoying life!).

PEELING POTATOES

Before peeling new potatoes, soak them in cold,
salted water for thirty minutes. They will peel
more easily and won't stain your hands.

● ● ●

END LEFTOVER BOREDOM

Don't throw away your leftovers! Use leftover chicken,
chili, beans, and more to create tasty burritos.
Your family will love this tasty new twist.

UNIFORM HAMBURGER PATTIES

To make uniform hamburger patties, find a jar lid of the desired
size and wash it well. Pack the lid tightly with ground beef,
smooth the top with a knife, turn it over, tap out the patty. . .
and voilà! Beautifully shaped hamburgers!

● ● ●

IT'S THE SIMPLE THINGS

Bake an extra pan of lasagna and deliver it to a family in
need. Sometimes the simplest things in life
mean the most.

ICE CUBE SKIMMER

When you find yourself with a skim of grease on the top of your soup or broth, place an ice cube on a slotted spoon and skim it over the grease. The grease will harden and stick to the spoon and the ice.

● ● ●

LIFE IS GOOD

Make a list of all the things for which you're thankful.
Write it on pretty stationery and display it on
the refrigerator where you'll see it often—a
daily reminder of everything that's good in
your life.

EVERYDAY BEAUTY

Place some fresh-cut flowers in a beautiful glass
vase on your tabletop. This is an easy way to bring
pure and simple delight to your dining room.

● ● ●

SLIPPERY CUTTING BOARD?

Keep your cutting board from sliding around on the countertop by cutting a piece of non-skid shelf liner to fit under the board.

COLD LEMONS?

Ever notice how a cold lemon doesn't like to give up its juice?
Microwave a lemon for ten to twenty seconds
before trying to squeeze it.

● ● ●

BAKED SWEET POTATOES

Baked sweet potatoes are a nice diversion from the average. Their sweetness is enticing to picky eaters. Serve topped with your choice of butter, cinnamon, brown sugar, mini marshmallows, and pecans. Kids will love piling on the flavors.

MINI MEASUREMENTS

To easily measure small amounts of liquid, use a medicine
dropper with measurements marked on the sides.

● ● ●

STOCK UP!

Cut down on the number of times you have to run to the store by stocking up a six-month supply of all nonperishable items. You'll be amazed at how much time you'll save!

SOUP KNOW-HOW

There's an old saying "Soup boiled is soup spoiled."
Always cook your soups gently and evenly.

● ● ●

ONION ODOR REMOVER

Remove onion odor from your hands by rubbing them with a paste of salt and vinegar.

CHICKEN COATING

You can easily coat chicken by placing it, along with flour and
seasoning mixture, into a brown lunch bag and shaking.

● ● ●

DINNER WITH A VIEW

A great stress reliever is to enjoy your food someplace other than the kitchen. Get out there and try dinner with a view of the sunset, in front of a blazing fire, on the front porch during a rain shower, or in the woods on a soft picnic blanket.

GRILLING

When grilling meat, don't pierce it with a fork or knife.
That will release the juices, and your meat will dry out.

● ● ●

SIMPLIFIED GROCERY LIST

Simplify your life by posting your grocery list on the refrigerator. Anytime a family member uses up the last of something, they're responsible for adding it to the list.

SIFTING DRY INGREDIENTS

When you don't have the time or patience for sifting
and just need to blend your dry ingredients, place all dry
ingredients in a small bowl and blend with a wire whisk.

● ● ●

CANDY BAR CRUSHING

You can easily crush candy bars by freezing them first.
Then place them in a resealable bag and break
them with a rolling pin.

NON-STICK CAKE TRICK

When you take a cake from the oven, place it on a
water-soaked towel for very short time. The cooled
cake will turn out of the pan without sticking.

● ● ●

SPICE CONTAINERS

Reuse a large spice container with the removable shaker shield. Fill the container with flour and label it clearly. Use the flour to dust your greased baking pans.

HOMEMADE PAN COATING

Make your own pan coating: Mix equal parts shortening, vegetable oil, and flour. Mix thoroughly and store, covered, in the refrigerator. Use this mixture at room temperature to coat baking pans instead of a spray or other method. It works wonders!

● ● ●

PRAYER. . .AND DESSERT!

Gather your family together once a week for devotions and dessert. Read through a family-friendly devotional book or study a passage from the Bible. End with prayer and a sweet treat!

GREASING PANS MADE EASY!

Make greasing a pan with shortening mess-free by placing
a plastic sandwich bag over your hand before spreading the
shortening onto the pan. When finished, just throw the bag away.

● ● ●

NATURAL ODOR ABSORBER

Baking soda naturally absorbs odors from spices and other items that give off an odor. As soon as you bring baking soda home from the store, place it in an airtight container. Even unopened, over time the cardboard box can allow the baking soda to become tainted.

CHOCOLATE CURLS
FROM SCRATCH

To make chocolate curls, use a block of chocolate at room temperature. Hold it in your hands for a while to warm it up. Once the chocolate is the proper temperature, run a vegetable peeler across the side of the bar, using moderate pressure, to produce curls. If you've never made chocolate curls before, you'll have to practice a few times to get it right; but once you see the end result, you'll agree that it's worth the extra work.

● ● ●

FROZEN BERRIES

If you choose to use frozen berries in your pies, first toss them with a sugar mixture while frozen. Allow them to sit for fifteen to thirty minutes, until partially thawed, before transferring them to a crust-lined pie plate.

DINNER AND FAMILY ENTERTAINMENT

Have a dinner-and-a-movie night with your family.
Make a simple dish, and gather everyone in the living room
to enjoy dinner while watching a family-friendly movie.

FANCY PUNCH BOWL

To dress up your punch bowl, float slices of orange
and pineapple in the bowl. If desired,
add maraschino cherries.

QUICK APPETIZER

For a quick, sweet appetizer, split open whole
dates and stuff a large piece of walnut in each.
Coat the dates in white granulated sugar and serve
to your guests as they wait for the main course.

● ● ●

CHOCOLATE AND COFFEE

Chocolate and coffee go well together. Create a welcoming atmosphere in your home by placing an aromatic candle—vanilla is a favorite—in a bowl or a jar. Fill the space around the candle with whole coffee beans up to an inch from the top of the candle. Then drink coffee and eat chocolate by candlelight.

KNOW A CHOCOLATE LOVER?

A great gift for a chocolate lover is a basket filled with chocolaty treats, such as a variety of candy bars, brownies with fudge icing, truffles, a German chocolate cake mix, fudge, chocolate syrup, an instant chocolate pudding mix, chocolate-covered pretzels, a hot cocoa mix. The possibilities are endless!

● ● ●

Cooking is like love. It should be entered into with abandon or not at all.

HARRIET VAN HORNE

A GIFT THAT KEEPS
ON GIVING

For a gift that keeps on giving, buy a cookie jar and fill it with
your home-baked cookies. You can even include the recipe.
Wrap up the jar in gift-wrap.

● ● ●

MAILING COOKIES

When preparing cookies to mail, use plastic wrap to
package cookies in pairs, back-to-back.

KIDS' SNACK MIX

When making snack mix. . .allow your kids to create a snack
mix of their own—adding ingredients of their choice. They'll
get a kick out of using their creative genius in the kitchen.
And they just might surprise you with a tasty treat!

● ● ●

BASKET GIFT CONTAINERS

Baskets are great containers for your baked-good gifts.
You can line a basket with shredded paper or a
kitchen towel. Tie a bright bow on the handle.
The entire basket can be covered in cellophane
and topped with a cascading bow.

TOASTY DIPS

Place dips in a small Crock-Pot to keep warm
while serving to party guests.

● ● ●

VEGGIE CHOPPING EFFICIENCY

When you're using your food processor, chop or grate several vegetables at once. Chopped celery, green pepper, and onion can then be stored in tightly sealed bags in the freezer until needed for a recipe.

NEW RECIPES AND FRIENDS

Invite your friends over for a night of recipe sharing. Have each person bring a covered dish (preferably from different categories)—so you'll have a salad, soup, bread, side dish, main dish, and dessert. Enjoy the meal and conversation. Be sure to have the various recipes written out on cards beforehand so everyone leaves with new dishes to try at home.

● ● ●

• • •

SIMPLE PLEASURES

Take time in your day to be inspired by something small—
the scent of a flower from your garden, a hug
from a child, an "I love you" from your
spouse. . . Then thank God for the little things
in life.

KID-FRIENDLY KITCHEN

Make your kitchen kid-friendly by stocking up on plastic
measuring cups, spoons, and mixing bowls. Personalize them
with a permanent marker. Your children will love using their
own kitchen tools when they help you prepare snacks and meals.

● ● ●

FRESH HERBS

Some grocery stores don't offer many fresh herbs beyond parsley. Dried herbs work well, though, in most all recipes. Just remember, if a recipe calls for a fresh herb, 1 tablespoon of fresh equals only 1 teaspoon of dried. When you want that fresh herb look, toss in some chopped parsley, adding color and texture without disturbing the balance of taste.

SIMPLE GESTURES

If you're the first person to arrive home in the afternoon, make an effort to greet your family members at the door with a smile! This simple gesture will make them feel loved and appreciated.

● ● ●

UNDER-RIPE FRUIT

Under-ripe peaches, pears, or nectarines can foil your
recipe plans. Try slicing the fruit and placing it
in a saucepan with apple or orange juice.
Add a bit of cinnamon and simmer the fruit
in juice for five minutes. Chill and add to your
recipe.

BUSY, BUSY!

If you're like most busy women, you barely have time to yourself
between work, running from here to there and back again with
the kids, piles of laundry, and those 101 other things you need
to accomplish all in twenty-four hours' time. When you're
feeling stressed, recite the following verse and feel the tension
melt away—*"Peace I leave with you; my peace I give you. I do not
give to you as the world gives. Do not let your hearts be troubled"*
(John 14:27).

● ● ●

FAVORITE RECIPES

Purchase a three-ring binder and use plastic photograph
sheets with six slots to organize and protect
your recipe collection. This is an easy and
inexpensive way to save yourself time in the
kitchen.

TEAMWORK

Have your family members pitch in and help at dinnertime.
Everyone gets a different assignment. If you cook the meals
every night, make someone else responsible for setting the table
and another person in charge of cleanup. With everyone
helping out, dinnertime won't seem like such a chore.

● ● ●

Our life is frittered away by detail. . . .
Simplify, simplify.

HENRY DAVID THOREAU

The qualitites of an exceptional cook are akin to those of a successful tightrope walker: an abiding passion for the task, courage to go out on a limb, and an impeccable sense of balance.

BRYAN MILLER

● ● ●

CELEBRATE TOGETHERNESS

Make it a priority to include your entire family around
the table for dinner at least one night a week.
Discuss each other's activities of the day and
revel in the warmth this togetherness brings to
your heart.

Enjoy the little things, for one day you may look
back and discover they were the big things.

<small>UNKNOWN</small>

● ● ●

MELTING CHOCOLATE

Chocolate has a very low melting point. It doesn't do well at excessively high heats (so be careful how long you bake your chocolate chip cookies). Always melt chocolate in a double boiler over very low heat, not letting the water boil.

HOT DRINK DELIGHT

For a wonderful addition to a hot drink, try cinnamon sticks.
Even better, dip your cinnamon sticks in melted chocolate
and let them dry before using them to stir your drink.

● ● ●

BUSY WOMAN'S PRAYER

Lord, some days I feel like a failure. I'm so busy that I can't accomplish everything on my to-do list. Please remind me (daily!) that it's okay to be me. My family and friends love me just as I am. And so do you, Lord. Thank You for loving each one of us in spite of our imperfections. Amen.

The discovery of a new dish does more for the
happiness of mankind than the discovery of a star.

ANTHELME BRILLAT-SAVARIN

● ● ●

BLOSSOMS ANYTIME

Buy some spring bulbs for daffodils, tulips, or hyacinths, and put them in the coldest corner of your refrigerator for two to four weeks. Fill over half a bucket or large vase with gravel, pebbles, or marbles. Nestle the bulbs among the top pebbles, points facing upward. Add water just to the tops of the pebbles. In a few weeks there will be blossoms for all to enjoy.

Simplicity is the ultimate sophistication.

Leonardo da Vinci (1452–1519)

● ● ●

CHEESE BOARD

Give a gift that keeps on giving. Buy a smooth, very nice piece of maple wood—a one-inch-thick board eight to ten inches wide. Cut it so that you have a square. Sand the rough edges. Seal with a quality sealant. Give the cheese board with your best cheese ball and a cheese knife or spreader.

WREATHS—NOT JUST
FOR DECORATION

Make an edible wreath. Create a ring of green grape bunches
on a plate. Add a few accents of red grapes or cherries.
You can even add a bow!

● ● ●

SMART COOKIE STORAGE

Baking a variety of cookies? Be sure to store each properly. Don't store your moist bars with your crisp cookies. Soft cookies should be stored in an airtight container. Crisp cookies do well under a loose-fitting cover that allows moisture to escape. Bar cookies can be cut when cooled and kept in their baking pan under a foil cover until you are ready to serve them.

QUICK TABLECLOTH

Use a colorful quilt to decorate your table.

● ● ●

NO-STICK COOKIE CUTTER TRICK

Lightly coat cookie cutters—especially plastic ones—
with oil spray to keep them from sticking to
the cookie dough.

SPIRITUAL RENEWAL

Create some time for daily spiritual renewal.
Relax in your favorite chair with hot tea,
your Bible, a devotional, and a simple treat. Enjoy!

● ● ●

FOOD AND BOOKS!

Read a fun, food-themed storybook with your kids—there are lots to choose from, covering everything from cookies to pancakes. When you've finished reading the story, prepare that particular food with your children. They will always remember this special time spent with you.

"Therefore I tell you, do not worry about your life,
what you will eat or drink."

MATTHEW 6:25

● ● ●

GREAT DINNER CONVERSATION

Write out a variety of questions on individual strips of
paper before placing in a conversation-starter
jar on the dinner table. Include questions
like: What's your favorite birthday memory?
If you could travel to any place in the world,
where would it be? And so on. Each night, have
a different family member pull a question from
the jar. You're guaranteed to liven up the dinner
table conversation!

JAR MIXES

Jar mixes are pretty because of their layers, but you can further dress up your canning jar gifts by cutting a piece of calico fabric with pinking shears to fit under the lid ring. You can also add multiple ribbons to the lid to hold the recipes. If you feel you need more embellishments, you can paint the outside of the jar with craft paint or the inside of the jar with melted chocolate.

● ● ●

DON'T FORGET THE. . .

Before heading to the grocery store, be sure to write out a list of what you need—rather than just making a mental note of it. As you go through the store, cross off items on your list as you place them in the cart. While this may seem like a lot of trouble, this definitely cuts down on those "Oh no, I forgot. . . !" moments. We've all been there!

Ponder well on this point:
The pleasant hours of our life are all connected
by a more or less tangible link with some
memory of the table.

CHARLES PIERRE MONSELET

TURN YOUR THOUGHTS TO THANKS

Do you find that you spend too much time worrying about what you just *have* to get done? Intentionally redirect your thoughts toward gratitude. What are you most thankful for? Your health? A loving family? A great career? You'll quickly forget about your worries when you see how richly the Lord has blessed you.

THE MEASUREMENTS CHEAT SHEET

½ tablespoon = 1½ teaspoons
1 tablespoon = 3 teaspoons
¼ cup = 4 tablespoons
⅓ cup = 5 tablespoons +
    1 teaspoon
½ cup = 8 tablespoons
½ pint = 1 cup (or 8 fluid ounces)
1 pint = 2 cups (or 16 fluid ounces)

1 quart = 4 cups (or 2 pints or
    32 ounces)
1 gallon = 16 cups (or 4 quarts)
1 pound = 16 ounces
1 peck = 8 quarts
1 bushel = 4 pecks

GIVE IT AWAY!

Give the stresses of your day to God. He wants you to!

CRAFTY APRON!

Create a personalized gift to give.
Buy a fabric apron and fabric paint.
Write the recipient's name and decorate the apron with paint.

● ● ●

A good meal makes a man feel
more charitable toward the world
than any sermon.

ARTHUR PENDENYS